ABOUT THE AUTHOR:
ELEANOR CREWES IS A LONDON-BASED
ILLUSTRATOR AND AUTHOR WHO GRADUATED
FROM THE UNIVERSITY OF THE ARTS LONDON.

THE DRAWINGS IN THIS BOOK WERE RENDERED USING
PALOMINO BLACKWING PEARL PENCILS.

the times I knew I was gay
by
Eleanor Crewes

virago

VIRAGO

First published in Great Britain in 2018 by Good Comics
This expanded edition published in 2020 by Virago Press

3 5 7 9 10 8 6 4

A CIP catalogue record for this book
is available from the British Library.

ISBN 978-0-349-01321-3

Printed and bound in Great Britain by Clays Ltd, Elcograf S.p.A.

Papers used by Virago are from well-managed forests
and other responsible sources.

MIX
Paper from
responsible sources
FSC® C104740

Virago Press
An imprint of
Little, Brown Book Group
Carmelite House
50 Victoria Embankment
London EC4Y 0DZ

An Hachette UK Company
www.hachette.co.uk

www.virago.co.uk

For my family and for T,
'What can't we face if we're together?'

'We form ourselves within the vocabularies that we did not choose, and sometimes we have to reject those vocabularies, or actively develop new ones.'
— Judith Butler, 2015

'People', the doctor said sadly, 'are always so anxious to get things out in the open where they can put a name to them.'
— Shirley Jackson, *The Haunting of Hill House*

'She scissored the curls away, and ... it was not like she was cutting hair, it was as if I had a pair of wings beneath my shoulder-blades, that the flesh had all grown over, and she was slicing free ...'
— Sarah Waters, *Tipping the Velvet*

the times I knew I was gay

A Note from The Author

In 2017 I stood by a large printer in one of the tech rooms at my university, and watched as orange paper began to emerge from its mouth.

The Times I Knew I Was Gay was an idea that sprang into my head just after I came out. What started as a secret project turned into a ten-page zine, with an orange cover. Like my own personal courier, I biked across London to deliver my zines to comic shops, posting them as close as Brighton and as far as Glasgow. Although the scale of the operation was modest, it quickly turned into something much bigger than I could fit into those hand-stitched comics.

This memoir has evolved in lots of ways over time, and what you hold here is its third and final edition. The artwork has developed throughout, a lot like my own coming out. The most recent drawings show a bolder, more confident line than the older ones, which are rougher and less sure. This is not a judgement on either style, or on either version of myself. As a queer writer, it was important to me that all evolutions of this book were preserved in some way, and I'm happy that they are together in one place for you to see.

This is not a handbook for coming out, or for being gay. But I like to think that if I had found this book as a child, or a teenager, or a young adult, I might have known a little more about myself a little sooner.

PROLOGUE

Growing up, I felt like I had a secret deep inside me.
It was as though someone had handed me a letter
that I had to keep very safe
but wasn't allowed to open
until the time was right.

I carried it around for years,
waiting for a sign that would tell me:
'It's now, you're ready.'

Until that moment I needed to be
the best version of myself at all times.
I needed to deserve my letter because, in my mind,
it held the secret to happiness.

ONE

GROWING UP,
I LOVED BEING DIFFERENT.

UNLIKE MOST OF THE GIRLS IN MY CLASS,
I LIKED GOTHS, ROCK MUSIC AND ANYTHING SPOOKY.

I INSISTED ON WEARING TROUSERS TO MY FIRST HOLY COMMUNION CEREMONY. (THIS DIDN'T GET A GREAT RECEPTION)

BUT I ALWAYS HAD MY BEST FRIENDS,
CAT, DAN AND CECILIA, TO UNDERSTAND ME.

WHEN WE WERE TEN, CECILIA SHOWED ME *BUFFY THE VAMPIRE SLAYER.*

I WAS HOOKED.

ANY MOMENT I COULD SNATCH
TO CHAT TO CECILIA ABOUT IT,
I WOULD.

I QUICKLY BECAME OBSESSED WITH THE
SPELL-CASTING, RED-HAIRED WILLOW ROSENBERG.

WILLOW BEGAN TO PLAY A ROLE IN MOST PARTS OF MY LIFE. PLAYING MAKE-BELIEVE AT SCHOOL, I WOULD ALWAYS CHOOSE TO BE CALLED 'WILLOW' AND I HAD MY LONG RED HAIR CHOPPED TO MY SHOULDERS EXACTLY LIKE HERS (THINK SEASON 3, 'DOPPLEGANGLAND').

SHE'S NOT ACTUALLY A VAMPIRE, BUT THIS IS A DOUBLE FROM ANOTHER DIMENSION

IN SEASON 4 WILLOW CAME OUT AND BEGAN A
RELATIONSHIP WITH TARA. WHEN I WATCHED
THIS WITH MY FAMILY WE DIDN'T TOTALLY
ACKNOWLEDGE THEIR RELATIONSHIP
BEYOND THE CONFINES OF MY TELEVISION.

ALTHOUGH I DID SIT IN MY ROOM AND
DRAW A LOT OF COMICS ABOUT THEM...

TWO

WHEN I WAS ELEVEN I MOVED FROM MY SMALL, ROSY-CHEEKED, CATHOLIC PRIMARY SCHOOL TO A VERY LARGE, VERY NOISY SECONDARY SCHOOL.

I WAS CATAPULTED FROM BEING IN THE OLDEST
CLASS TO BEING IN THE YOUNGEST,
AND I FELT VERY YOUNG.

IN PRIMARY SCHOOL I THOUGHT I WAS COOL, SO IN CHARGE. BUT SUDDENLY ALL THE THINGS I LIKED, OTHER PEOPLE MADE FUN OF.

I DIDN'T LIKE BEING JUDGED, SO I TRIED TO SHOW OFF
A TOUGH EXTERIOR, A BARRIER THAT SAID:
'DON'T MESS WITH ME!'

BUT THAT TOUGH PERSONA BROKE DOWN WHEN I WAS TEASED. LIKE WHEN I WORE THE TRAINING BRA I'D BEEN SO PROUD OF.

I HAD FELT REALLY COOL WHEN MY OLD FRIENDS HAD SEEN IT.

SUDDENLY MY BRA SEEMED SO CHILDISH,
SO SMALL AND SILLY.

I CLEARLY WASN'T VERY GOOD AT BEING GROWN UP!

I WAS PRETTY SCARED OF BEING REJECTED SO I TOOK MY FEARS OUT ON MY FRIENDS.

IT MADE ME FEEL TERRIBLE.

SCHOOL HAD BECOME SUCH A CONFUSING
PLACE THAT COME SUMMER I COULDN'T WAIT
TO HEAD OFF TO MY FAMILY IN ITALY
AND FORGET ABOUT IT ALL FOR A FEW MONTHS.

IN ITALY I COULD TOTALLY RELAX INTO MYSELF.
THERE WERE NO FRIENDS OR PEERS
OBSERVING ME, ONLY MY FAMILY.

AWAY FROM TEENAGE COMPETITIVENESS,
ITALY WAS A PLACE WHERE MY BROTHER AND I
COULD JUST BE KIDS.

BACK IN LONDON, SCHOOL STILL HUNG OVER ME LIKE A HEAVY CLOUD, TO THE POINT WHERE I STARTED BEGGING NOT TO HAVE TO GO BACK.

I FELT AS THOUGH I HAD TWO SELVES:
ONE WAS THE PERSON I NEEDED TO BE
WITH MY NEW FRIENDS,
AND THE OTHER WAS WHO I HAD ALWAYS BEEN
WITH MY OLD FRIENDS AND MY FAMILY.

THERE WAS SOMETHING THAT DIDN'T
FEEL RIGHT, BUT I CHOSE
TO IGNORE IT.

I WAS TERRIFIED OF BULLIES,
THE WAY THEY SEEMED TO READ YOUR MIND,
OR SEE YOU MORE CLEARLY THAN YOU
SAW YOURSELF.

AND THAT WAS REALLY SCARY.

THERE WAS ONE BOY IN PARTICULAR AT MY SCHOOL,
WHO WAS ALWAYS PICKED ON FOR BEING GAY.

IT QUICKLY TURNED FROM A RUMOUR INTO A FACT, AND THIS TERRIFIED ME THE MOST.

EVERYONE SEEMED SO HUNGRY TO KNOW
EVERYTHING ABOUT YOU.

AND I DIDN'T EVEN SEEM TO KNOW MYSELF ANY MORE.

I HID AWAY IN THE LIBRARY.

WHATEVER ANYONE FOUND OUT ABOUT ME,
AT LEAST I HAD MY FRIENDS TO TELL.

THREE

AS CAT, AISLING AND I GOT OLDER IT
SUDDENLY SEEMED LIKE EVERYONE
HAD BOYFRIENDS.

IN PRIMARY SCHOOL I HAD LOVED THE SAME BOY FOR MANY YEARS BUT I HADN'T REALLY FANCIED ANYONE. A WHOLE NEW WORLD WAS OPENING UP BEFORE ME AND I DIDN'T KNOW WHETHER TO DIVE IN OR RUN FOR THE HILLS.

THE FLIRTING TECHNIQUES OF A (UNBEKNOWNST TO HER) CLOSETED LESBIAN.

STEP ONE:

BECOME THE BOY — MAKE A NOTE OF HIS HAIRCUT, TRAINERS, RUCKSACK, HOW MANY WRISTBANDS HE WEARS / WHAT COLOUR THEY ARE. DOES HE HAVE A NECKLACE? IS IT ONE OF THOSE WOODEN BEADED ONES FROM TOPMAN? YES? GOOD — THEY'RE CHEAP AND EASILY ATTAINABLE.

STEP TWO:

WHAT TV SHOWS DOES HE WATCH? ARE THEY AT BLOCKBUSTER? CAN I WATCH AN ENTIRE SERIES IN ONE WEEKEND AND THEREFORE BE ABLE TO MAKE CONVERSATION ON MONDAY IN HISTORY?

AM I VERGING ON BECOMING A STALKER? NO!
I'M FLIRTING, SOWING THE SEED, GETTING A FEEL FOR
THE LAY OF THE LAND.

STEP THREE:

AS SOON AS I KNOW THAT THEY FANCY ME BACK, DECIDE THAT IT'S TOO STRESSFUL AND WHAT YOU'VE NOW BUILT AS FRIENDSHIP IS TOO VALUABLE TO LOSE.

THE FIRST BOY I SAID I
FANCIED* WAS IN YEAR 8.

WE BOTH LIKED READING
MANGA AND WATCHING
ANIME AND WOULD TALK
OBSESSIVELY ABOUT OUR
FAVOURITE STORY LINES.

*WHEN I SAY 'FANCY',
IT MEANT MORE
BECAUSE THEY LIKED
THE SAME THINGS AS ME.
I THOUGHT THAT THE
PHYSICAL ATTRACTION
WOULD COME LATER ON.

HE TOOK ME ON MY FIRST EVER DATE TO WATCH
STARDUST AT THE ODEON CINEMA.
WE DIDN'T SPEAK THE WHOLE TIME BUT THAT
DIDN'T STOP ME FROM ASKING HIM TO BE
MY BOYFRIEND VIA MSN INSTANT MESSENGER.

WE DIDN'T SPEAK AFTER THAT EITHER.
AFTER TWO WEEKS OF BEING A 'COUPLE'
CAT AND AISLING BROKE UP WITH HIM FOR ME.

THE SECOND BOY I REALLY FANCIED WENT TO A
DIFFERENT SCHOOL.

HE WAS SMART — COOL!
HE WAS JEWISH — COOL!
AND HE FANCIED ME BACK — MEGA COOL!

I HAD MY FIRST KISS WITH HIM WHEN I WAS FOURTEEN
AT THE CINEMA (THE SAME ONE I'D WATCHED
STARDUST AT IN YEAR 8). I WAS SO AWARE
OF HIM FROM THE MOMENT WE SAT DOWN
IN FRONT OF THE SCREEN.

AS THE FILM PLAYED WE MOVED
CLOSER AND CLOSER TOGETHER.

AS WE KISSED I FELT SO MANY THINGS!

WHAT'S THE PERSON NEXT TO US THINKING? CAN CAT AND CECILIA SEE US? IS THIS NICE??!
WHEN DO WE STOP?!
SLURRRP

THE CLOSER WE GOT, THE MORE STRESSED OUT I BECAME, UNTIL I FINALLY DUMPED HIM OVER MSN.

WHEN I WAS SIXTEEN, I GOT INTO MY FIRST REAL RELATIONSHIP. NOT SOME SILENT EXCHANGE OF MANGA, OR COVERT KISSING IN THE CINEMA, BUT A PROPER RELATIONSHIP. TALKS ABOUT *EMOTIONS*. DINNERS WITH PARENTS. *SLEEPOVERS*. IN THE *SAME BED*.

BUT FOR ALL THE 'REALNESS' I THOUGHT THIS
RELATIONSHIP HAD, WE WERE STILL JUST TWO
SIXTEEN YEAR OLDS FIGURING THINGS OUT.

I LIKED TALKING ABOUT SEX WITH CAT AND AISLING.
WHEN WE SPOKE IT FELT SO ATTAINABLE,
SO NORMAL AND EXCITING.

NO MATTER HOW MUCH TIME HE AND I SPENT
KISSING AND FUMBLING THROUGH
OUR TEENAGE HORMONES, I COULDN'T
HAVE SEX WITH HIM.

I FELT SO ISOLATED.
I KNEW PEOPLE WHO HADN'T HAD SEX, BUT
THAT WAS BECAUSE THEY HADN'T HAD
BOYFRIENDS YET. IT SEEMED THAT NO ONE
WHO HAD A BOYFRIEND WAS STILL A VIRGIN.

IT GOT TO THE POINT WHERE I WAS SO
DISTRESSED AND CONFUSED I SPOKE TO MY
MUM ABOUT IT.

WE BROKE UP AFTER A YEAR.
I SPENT ABOUT A WEEK AVOIDING HIM AT SCHOOL,
CRYING IN THE TOILETS WHEN I NEEDED TO
AND THEN I GOT OVER IT.

THE ONLY THING LEFT WAS TO FIND MYSELF AGAIN.
WHEN WE'D BEEN TOGETHER I'D CHANGED
SO MUCH.

BREAKING THE FOURTH WALL HERE: AUTOBIOGRAPHIES ARE HARD BECAUSE IT MEANS LOOKING BACK AND TRYING TO FIGURE STUFF OUT — I KNOW WHO I AM NOW, BUT WHO WAS I THEN? AND QUEER MEMOIR IS PARTICULARLY HARD!

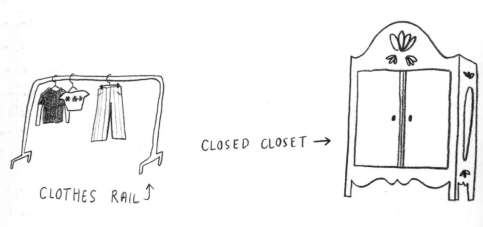

CLOSED CLOSET →

CLOTHES RAIL ↑

PEOPLE MIGHT THINK THAT EVERYONE STARTS OUT IN A CLOSET UNTIL THEY'RE READY TO 'COME OUT'. THE CLOSET COULD BE DARK AND SCARY OR QUITE ROOMY AND RESEMBLE MORE OF A CLOTHES RAIL. BUT WHAT'S FUNNY FOR ME IS THAT I DIDN'T EVEN KNOW THAT THERE WAS A CLOSET — OR THAT I WAS VERY MUCH STUCK INSIDE IT.

FOUR

IT STARTED WITH RUNNING.

I WANTED TO REINVENT MYSELF.

BUT THAT DESIRE LED ME DOWN SOME DARK PATHS.

A DETERMINATION TO
GO FURTHER,
EAT LESS,
GET THINNER,
BE BETTER,
LOOK SEXIER,
BE DESIRABLE,
BE *DESERVING.*

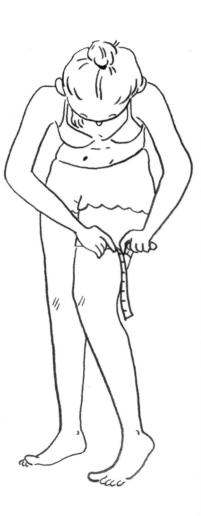

FROM THE AGE OF FOURTEEN UNTIL I WAS ABOUT
TWENTY I WAS HOLDING IN MY STOMACH.

I WAS SO TENSE ALL THE TIME.
I WAS PHYSICALLY FORCING MYSELF INTO AN IDENTITY
THAT WASN'T MINE.

101

WITHOUT REALISING, I WAS STARTING TO CONTROL EVERYTHING ABOUT MY APPEARANCE, IDENTITY AND LOVE LIFE.

I WANTED TO MAKE SURE I ARRIVED AT UNIVERSITY AS A PROPER ADULT. I WAS SO DETERMINED TO BE OLDER, SKINNIER, COOLER!

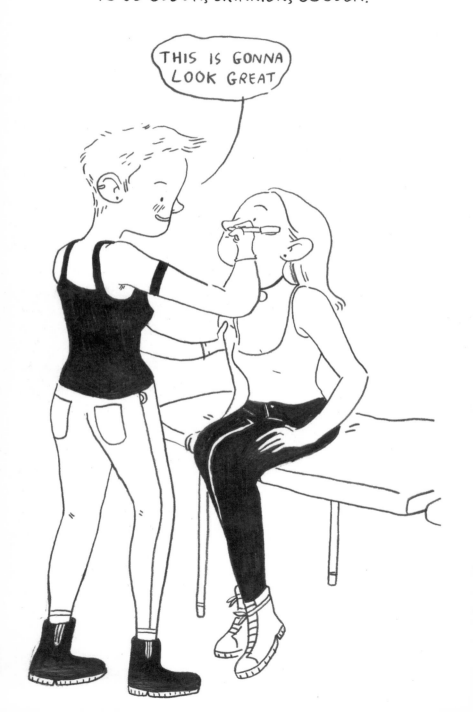

BUT MY STRUGGLE WITH FOOD WAS A SUBCONSCIOUS WAY TO REDIRECT MYSELF FROM THE FACT THAT I WAS GAY.

I CREATED A PROBLEM TO DISTRACT MY BODY FROM MY BRAIN, A PASTIME FUELLED WITH ANXIETY, BUT ONE THAT WAS EASIER TO RECKON WITH THAN ANY OF MY DEEPER, TRUER FEELINGS.

FIVE

WHEN I ARRIVED AT UNIVERSITY I FELT SO COOL.

I JUST COULDN'T HOLD ON TO THE PERSON I'D SPENT
SO MANY MONTHS PREPARING MYSELF TO BE.

IN MY HEAD I THOUGHT THAT BEING AT
UNIVERSITY WOULD LIFT AWAY THE THINGS THAT
HAD HELD ME BACK AT SECONDARY SCHOOL.
I WAS GOING TO BE A SOCIAL QUEEN,
I'D GO ON LOADS OF DATES AND MOST IMPORTANTLY
— I'D GET A BOYFRIEND.

MY FRIENDS AND I WOULD FRANTICALLY SCAN FACEBOOK, TRYING TO FIND THE HOTTEST BOYS ON OUR COURSE:

AAEEEEEEEE!!

JOHN FROM SURFACE DESIGN IS A DREAM!

AND EVEN THOUGH I JOINED IN ON THIS MANIC HUNT, I WAS ALWAYS DISAPPOINTED. THE PIXELATED AND CROPPED FACES FROM THE BACKLIGHT OF MY LAPTOP DID NOTHING FOR ME.

I JUST DIDN'T CARE.

I WANTED TO BE KISSED, JUST NOT BY ANY OF THEM!

I WAS NERVOUS.

IF I DIDN'T MEET SOMEONE AT UNIVERSITY, WHERE THE HELL WOULD I?

AND IF I WASN'T MEETING SOMEONE I LIKED, WHAT ABOUT SEX?

SEX WAS QUICKLY BECOMING MORE
AND MORE TERRIFYING THE CLEARER IT
BECAME THAT I DIDN'T LIKE ANY
OF THE BOYS ENOUGH.

BEING AT SECONDARY SCHOOL HAD
PROTECTED ME SOMEWHAT.
BUT AT UNIVERSITY I WAS AN ADULT,
AND ADULTS HAVE SEX.

THAT SUMMER
I BEGAN WORKING AS A KITCHEN
RUNNER AT A BAR IN SOHO.

I PRETTY MUCH HATED WORKING THERE.

WORKING AT THIS BAR I MET A WOMAN
CALLED ROSE.

DURING THE FIRST SHIFT I HAD WITH HER,
A MUCH OLDER CHEF LEANED OVER
THE COUNTER TO ME AND, NODDING
HIS HEAD TOWARDS ROSE,
BEGAN JAMMING HIS
FINGERS TOGETHER IN
A SCISSORING MOTION.

THE MEN IN THE KITCHEN WOULD OFTEN MAKE ME FEEL UNCOMFORTABLE.

ROSE NEVER SEEMED TO PAY ANY MIND TO THESE WORDS OR GESTURES, SHE BARELY LIFTED HER HEAD IN RESPONSE.

AND I ALSO NEVER SPOKE OUT.

THE OTHER CHEFS' LANGUAGE WOULD
PARALYZE ME, LEAVE MY MIND FLIPPING.
I FELT SO ANGRY FOR HER BUT ALSO SO WORRIED
THAT IT MIGHT REVEAL SOMETHING ABOUT
ME IF I DEFENDED HER.

IT WAS AS THOUGH I BLACKED OUT AT EVERY
MENTION OF THE WORD 'GAY' OR 'LESBIAN'.
MY MIND SIMPLY COULDN'T HANDLE IT.

A WEEK OR SO BEFORE I LEFT THAT JOB,
ROSE ALSO LEFT.

SHE ANNOUNCED IT QUITE SUDDENLY.
AT THE TIME I WAS SO SAD,
I COULDN'T IMAGINE NOT HAVING HER
DOWNSTAIRS WITH ME, SHOWING ME HOW TO
SNAP THE WATERCRESS SO IT SAT ON THE
PLATE NEATLY, TALKING ME THROUGH THE WAY
THE FRIDGE WAS ARRANGED.

AFTER SHE LEFT, THE FRIDGE BECAME A SHORT
ESCAPE FOR ME DURING THOSE SHIFTS.
A MOMENT TO DULL OUT THE SOUND OF THE
REGISTER SENDING DOWN ORDERS,
A MOMENT TO COLLECT MY THOUGHTS AND
NOT HAVE TO BE IN A ROOM
FULL OF MEN.

131

THESE WERE OLDER MEN WHO WILL NEVER KNOW BETTER. IT WAS SIMPLY THE FIRST TIME I HAD EXPERIENCED MEN (NOT TEENAGE BOYS) TAKING SOMETHING FROM ME THAT THEY'D ALREADY DECIDED WAS THEIRS TO TAKE.

SIX

NEW YEAR'S EVE 2013

CECILIA, CAT AND I WENT TO A FRIEND'S NEW YEAR'S EVE PARTY IN SOUTH LONDON. IT WAS A STRANGE MIXTURE OF PEOPLE I KNEW FROM PRIMARY SCHOOL, UP TO THOSE I'D MET AT UNIVERSITY.

SCENARIO:
I'M ABOUT TO COME OUT FOR THE
FIRST TIME.
DATE: 01/01/2014
TIME: 1.30 A.M.

I WENT TO SLEEP THAT NIGHT FEELING SO CONTENT,
SO CALM FOR THE FIRST TIME IN A WHILE.
I DON'T KNOW WHAT HAD HAPPENED DURING THAT
DAY TO HAVE BROUGHT THIS REALISATION INTO MY MIND

ALL I CAN PUT IT DOWN TO WAS THAT AFTER
YEARS OF TIRING MYSELF OUT WITH RULES
AND REGULATIONS, AN EVENING WITH MY
BEST FRIENDS MADE ME FEEL SO HAPPY AND
COMFORTABLE I FINALLY LET SOMETHING GO
AND THE TRUTH COME OUT.

WHATEVER HAD CAUSED THIS TO HAPPEN,
IT COULDN'T LAST.

THE NEXT MORNING I AWOKE TO ANOTHER DAY
OF HETERONORMATIVITY.

I DIDN'T COME OUT AGAIN FOR A LONG
TIME AFTER THAT.

STORIES YOU HEAR ABOUT PEOPLE COMING OUT ARE
OFTEN TOLD AS ONE BIG MOMENT. EVEN IF THE
BUILD-UP HAS BEEN LONG AND PAINFUL
– 'COMING OUT' IS FREQUENTLY
DESCRIBED AS A DEFINITIVE
AND SINGULAR THING.

BUT IT DIDN'T HAPPEN LIKE THAT FOR *ME*.

MY COMING OUT WASN'T JUST A ONE-TIME THING,
IT DIDN'T HAPPEN SO NEATLY.
AFTER THIS FIRST COMING OUT IN FRONT
OF DONNY OSMOND *AND HIS TECHNICOLOUR
DREAMCOAT*, IT TOOK ME TWO WHOLE
YEARS TO COME OUT AGAIN.

IN 2015 I CAME OUT ANOTHER FOUR TIMES,
WHICH WOULD MAKE IT A GRAND
TOTAL OF FIVE.

WHEN I WAS NINETEEN I HAD SEX.
WE MET AT A DINNER AND HE WAS REALLY NICE.

IN BED HE TOLD ME I WAS SEXY AND BEAUTIFUL
AND I SAID NOTHING.

AFTERWARDS HE GAVE ME HIS LAST CHOCOLATE
BISCUIT BAR.

THE NEXT DAY I FELT TWO THINGS:

ONE WAS THAT I COULDN'T WAIT TO TELL MY
FRIEND IN THE ROOM DOWN THE HALL.

AND TWO WAS THAT I DIDN'T FEEL ANYTHING
ROMANTIC TOWARDS HIM ANY MORE.

AT THE TIME I PUT MY CHANGE OF HEART DOWN TO
THE FACT THAT I SAW HIM IN SOCKS AND
FLIP-FLOPS.

IT WAS PRETTY COMMON FOR ME TO FIND SMALL,
SHALLOW REASONS NOT TO
HAVE THE HOTS FOR
A GUY ANY MORE.

IT COULD BE HIS NEW HAIRCUT,

OR THE FUZZY BEARD HE WAS TRYING TO GROW.

IN THE MOMENT THESE REASONS FELT
EXTREMELY VALID.

I'M JUST GONNA STEP IN HERE FOR A SECOND AND SAY I'M WELL AWARE I WAS DELUDING MYSELF.

I'D COME OUT AS GAY ABOUT TWO MONTHS BEFORE HAVING SEX WITH A GUY AND THEN CONTINUED TO DATE MEN AFTER THAT.
I JUST CLEARLY WASN'T READY TO BE HONEST.

SEVEN

A PANIC ATTACK STARTS WITH SHORTNESS OF BREATH.

OR AT LEAST IT DID FOR ME.

MY VISION BEGAN TO TUNNEL
AND MY BREATHING QUICKENED.

IT WAS LIKE SEEING RED —
NOT THE RED OF ANGER
BUT THE RED OF EMERGENCY,
FLASHING SIRENS
TELLING EVERYONE TO
'GET OUT OF THE WAY!'

I HADN'T SAVED MY COURSEWORK PROPERLY.

169

I'M GOING TO FAIL.

I'M GOING TO FAIL MY DEGREE
AND IF I FAIL I HAVE TO CONFRONT
WHY I FAILED AND IF I CONFRONT
MY FAILURE I'LL UNDERSTAND WHY
I'VE FOUGHT SO HARD NOT TO FAIL.

IN THOSE THIRTY SECONDS
OF RED, THE CONTROL I HAD
FORCED INTO MY MIND, MY
BODY AND UNDER MY SKIN
FINALLY BROKE.

THE DAY AFTER MY PANIC ATTACK I MADE THE DECISION TO SEE A COUNSELLOR.

AS I WENT TO BED THE NIGHT BEFORE
MY FIRST SESSION I TOOK A SMALL NOTEPAD
FROM MY DESK AND WROTE AT
THE TOP OF A PAGE
— 'THE WAVES ARE CRASHING AND CALLING.'

SEEING MY COUNSELLOR PULLED THOSE
WAVES BACK OUT TO SEA.

WE SPOKE ABOUT MY WORK AT UNIVERSITY,
MY FAMILY, THE WAY I FELT ABOUT MY BODY.
BUT I NEVER TOLD HER ABOUT THE FACT THAT
I HAD COME OUT AS GAY ON NEW YEAR'S EVE.

I DIDN'T TALK TO ANYONE ELSE ABOUT SEX, EITHER. SLEEPING WITH THAT GUY HADN'T OPENED UP THE WORLD OF SEX TO ME IN THE WAY I HAD EXPECTED. I WAS STILL VERY UNCOMFORTABLE WHEN CONFRONTED BY THE TOPIC.

I DID SPEAK TO THE COUNSELLOR ABOUT BOYS, THOUGH
I TOLD HER ABOUT GUYS THAT I THOUGHT WERE
NICE, BOYS THAT I FANCIED. BUT EVERY TIME SHE
ASKED ME HOW I REALLY FELT ABOUT IT ALL,
I'D BE HONEST AND SAY I DIDN'T REALLY CARE.

EIGHT

WHEN I MOVED INTO A FLAT WITH MY FRIENDS
I STARTED TO REALISE AGAIN THAT I WAS GAY.
I'D BECOME MORE SETTLED AT ART SCHOOL AND BEEN
EXPOSED TO A LOT MORE QUEER CULTURE THAN BEFOR

186

AT THAT TIME I MET SOMEONE WHO WAS
GOING THROUGH THE SAME PROCESS.
WE BECAME GOOD FRIENDS.

SHE HAD A BOYFRIEND BUT WE'D OFTEN TALK ABOUT
THE GIRLS THAT SHE LIKED.

WE'D SOMETIMES HOLD HANDS. I'D MEET
HER AFTER CLASS AND WE'D SPEND OUR
EVENINGS TOGETHER.

ONCE AGAIN,
I FELT LIKE I HAD TWO SELVES: THE PERSON I WAS
WHEN I WAS AT UNIVERSITY AND THE PERSON I WAS
WHEN I WAS WITH HER.

AT UNIVERSITY I'D TALK ABOUT BOYS WITH
GIRLS IN MY CLASS, SCROLL THROUGH TINDER,
AND SET UP DATES.

BUT WHEN WE WERE ALONE, IT FELT LIKE WE CREATED OUR OWN BUBBLE. WE CLOSED THE DOOR ON ANYONE WHO COULD POSSIBLY INTERFERE AND SPOKE ONLY ABOUT EACH OTHER AND WHAT WE COULD BE.

EVEN WITH THIS FRIENDSHIP HAPPENING IN THE
SIDELINES OF MY LIFE I STILL NEVER SAID THAT I WAS
GAY TO ANYONE ELSE. I THINK I WAS HOPING, MAYBE
WAITING, FOR HER TO BE READY TO SAY IT WITH ME.
TOGETHER.
BUT SHE CHOSE TO STAY WITH HER BOYFRIEND
AND I HAD TO COME OUT ALONE.

THE KNOWLEDGE BEGAN TO SOLIDIFY IN MY MIND
AND IT WOULD COME TO ME IN PRIVATE MOMENTS.

IT WASN'T SUCH AN EPIPHANY AS LAST TIME
WITH CAT AND CELI, IT WAS MORE LIKE

SMALL MOMENTS OF CLARITY,

LIKE I HAD TO TEST THE WORDS,
ALLOW THEM TO SETTLE INSIDE ME
BEFORE SPEAKING THEM ALOUD TO ANYONE ELSE.

NEAR THE END OF SUMMER, ONE AFTERNOON MY BROTHER CAME BY TO HELP ME START MOVING MY THINGS OUT OF MY ROOM.

OUR LEASE WAS ALMOST UP AND I WANTED TO MOVE BACK HOME.

AT THE SUPERMARKET WHILE BUYING OUR LUNCH,
I FELT READY,
FINALLY.

*MY BROTHER CALLS ME BIRD, BABY BIRD, BIRDUS, E-BIRD, B-BIRD, *UCCELLINA* (THAT'S ITALIAN FOR BABY GIRL BIRD).

TELLING HIM TURNED OUT TO BE EASIER
THAN TELLING MYSELF.

BUT FOR ALL MY EFFORTS I STILL FOUGHT
AGAINST IT.

NOT LONG AFTER THIS
I SWIPED RIGHT ON MY 'MR BIG'.

HE WAS *TALL!*
HE WAS *OLDER THAN ME!*
HE *ROCK CLIMBED!*
HE *HIKED!*
HE *COOKED!*
HE HAD A JOB!

HE WAS EVERYTHING I HAD
EVER SAID I WANTED IN A
BOYFRIEND SO I
COULDN'T NOT GIVE
IT A GO.

BUT I HAD A PLAN.
IF OUR DATE DIDN'T GO WELL THEN I WOULD
BE CERTAIN THAT I WAS GAY.

MY LAST HETERO DATE

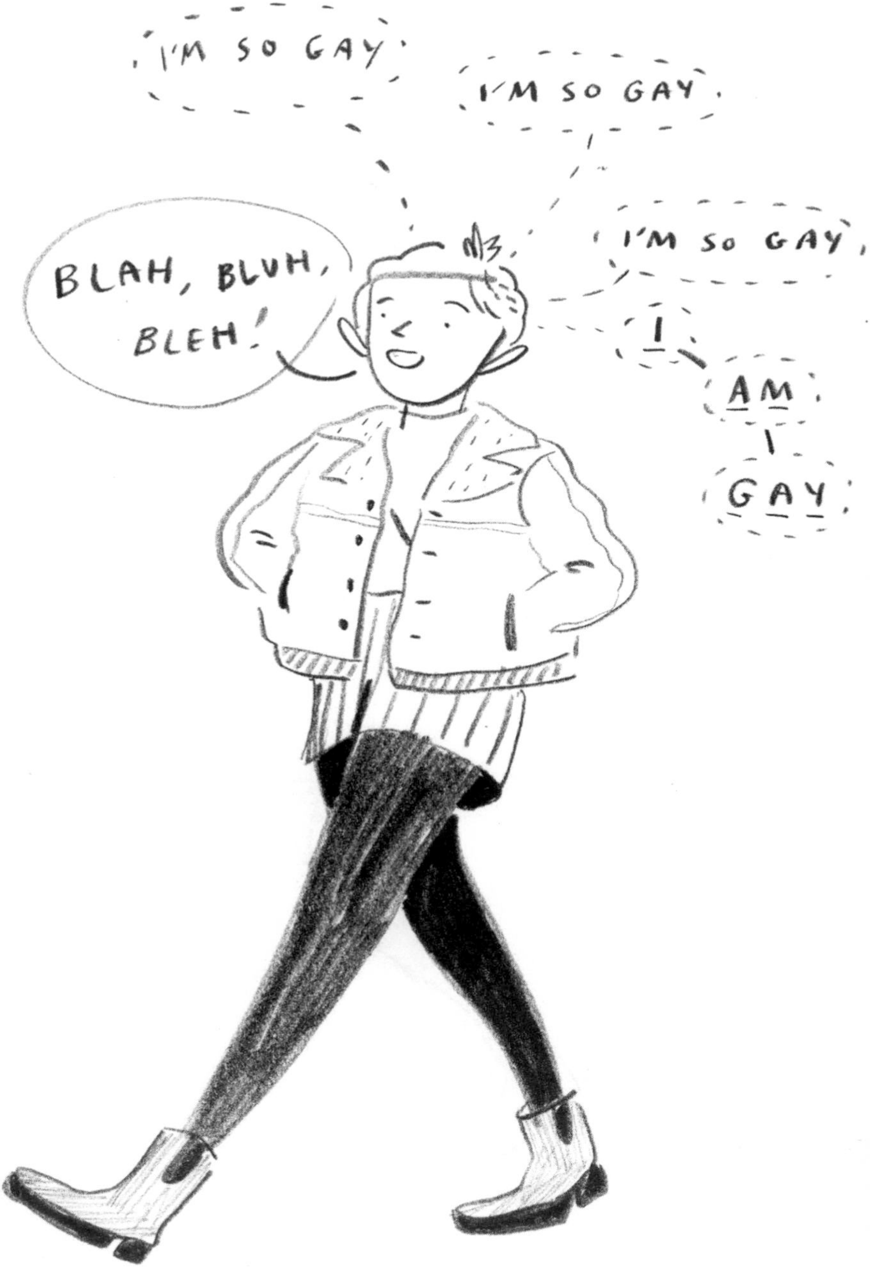
I'M SO GAY
I'M SO GAY
BLAH, BLUH, BLEH!
I'M SO GAY
I AM GAY

NINE

I REMEMBER THE MORNING AFTER THAT DATE
AND THE FEELING OF FINALLY KNOWING.
A DIFFERENT KNOWING THAN BEFORE. A DEFINITIVE
KNOWING, LIKE _THIS_ _IS_ _IT_.

MY PARENTS WERE AWAY AND THE HOUSE WAS QUIET.
MY BROTHER WAS STILL SLEEPING IN THE ROOM
NEXT DOOR, SO I WENT FOR IT.

'I'M GAY.'

IT WAS NEVER SOMETHING I'D SAID IN _MY HOUSE_ — I'D
ALWAYS BEEN SOMEWHERE ELSE: AT CECILIA'S, IN MY
FLAT, ON THE TUBE, ON THE STREET! I THREW THE
WORDS AROUND MY ROOM, A PLACE WHERE I HAD SLEPT
SINCE I WAS A BABY. THE WALLPAPER, DECORATIONS AND
BEDDING HAD CHANGED OVER THE YEARS BUT THIS
ROOM WAS _MINE_. IT HAD HOUSED ME OVER ALL THIS
TIME, SO IT FELT RIGHT THAT IT WAS THE FIRST TO KNOW

I LAY IN BED AND IMAGINED THE WORDS SQUEEZING OUT
FROM UNDER MY DOOR, FINDING THEMSELVES IN THE
HALLWAY AND SPLITTING OFF — SOME RAN INTO THE
BATHROOM AND LAID AGAINST THE COOL OF THE TILES,
OTHERS SLIPPED DOWNSTAIRS, SPILLING OVER THE
BANISTER AND SPLASHING UP THE WALLS OF MY
KITCHEN — THEY SPED INTO THE LIVING ROOM AND
PULLED OPEN THE BOOKS, TORE OUT THE WORDS AND
REPLACED THEM WITH ME. MY HOUSE AND I WERE
ROARING INTO NEW LIFE WHILE ALSO STAYING
EXACTLY THE SAME
— 'I'M GAY'.

217

TELLING MY HOUSE WASN'T SCARY,
IT COULDN'T TALK BACK.

I WAS NERVOUS ABOUT TELLING MY PARENTS, THOUGH.
IT WASN'T SOMETHING I'D EVER HAD TO PREPARE FOR
BECAUSE I'D NEVER HAD ANYTHING SOLID ENOUGH TO
TELL THEM. MY FEARS GREW FROM THE FEELING THAT
GAY WASN'T IN MY PARENTS' VOCABULARY. NOT BECAUS
THEY WERE AGAINST IT BUT BECAUSE THEY'D NEVER
LIVED WITH IT. GAY, QUEER, LGBT+ WAS NOT A PART OF
THEIR DAILY LIVES AND SO THEY HAD RAISED ME IN AN
UNCONSCIOUSLY HETEROSEXUAL ENVIRONMENT.

IT WAS LIKE WHEN WE WATCHED *BUFFY THE VAMPIRE SLAYER* — MY PARENTS AND I LOVED WILLOW AND TARA'S RELATIONSHIP. *BUFFY* WAS A COOL FANTASY WORLD THAT WE DIPPED INTO WEEKLY. THE CHARACTER WERE ACTION FIGURES, POSTERS, STICKERS, TOP TRUMPS AND PEOPLE I WOULD DRAW FOR MY OWN CHILDISH COMICS. BUT ONCE THE EPISODE WAS OVER W LEFT THE WORLD OF *BUFFY* AND WENT BACK TO 'NORMAL LIFE'.

WILLOW AND TARA WERE A PART OF THAT FICTIONAL WORLD, AND SO WAS THEIR RELATIONSHIP.

SO THOUGH I WAS DESPERATELY FINDING MYSELF IN EVERY ASPECT OF WILLOW, I NEVER EVEN CONSIDERED THAT THE BIGGEST PART OF HER CHARACTER — HER SEXUALITY — WAS THE MOST FUNDAMENTAL THING WE SHARED.

IT TURNED OUT THAT TELLING MY PARENTS WAS VERY EASY.

225

MY MUM AND I HAVE ALWAYS HAD A VERY TELEPATHIC RELATIONSHIP. IT'S FUNNY, BUT AT MOMENTS WHEN I'VE REALLY NEEDED HER, SHE'S READ MY MIND BEFORE I'VE EVEN SAID WHAT THE PROBLEM IS.

LIKE THAT TIME WHEN I WAS AN EMBARRASSED SIXTEEN YEAR OLD (PRE-EMPTIVE IN MY CONTRACEPTIVE REQUIREMENTS).

OR THAT TIME I HIT A ROAD BUMP AT HIGH SPEED, FLINGING MYSELF OFF THE BIKE AND BREAKING MY WRIST. IT LOOKED LIKE A POTATO.

AND THIS TIME WAS NO DIFFERENT.

AFTER THAT, TELLING THE REST OF MY
FAMILY WAS SIMPLE.

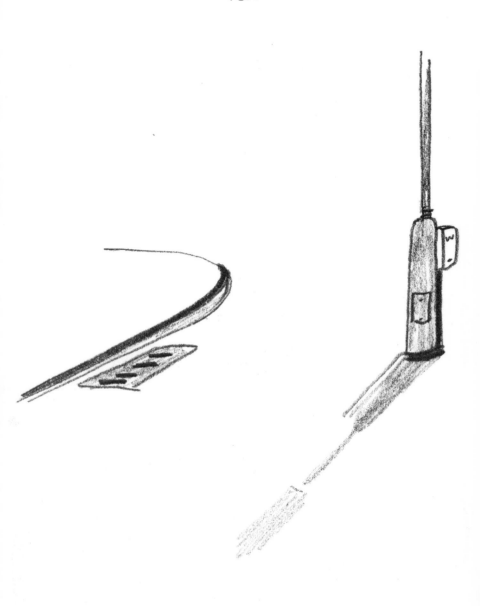

TEN

I FELT LIKE MY BODY WAS IN SHOCK.
ALL THE WAYS I HAD TRIED TO EXPRESS MYSELF
AND CONTROL MY IMAGE FELL AWAY BECAUSE
I HAD *FINALLY* TOLD THE TRUTH.

I SUDDENLY HAD THIS NEW BURST OF LIFE.
I WAS TWENTY-ONE WITH TWENTY-ONE YEARS OF
QUEER CULTURE TO CATCH UP ON — OH BABY!

I GOT TO LOOK AT MYSELF IN THIS WHOLE OTHER LIGHT.
THE ONE QUESTION I HAD WORRIED ABOUT AND TORN
MYSELF UP OVER WAS *ANSWERED!*

I STILL FLIPPED AROUND A LOT FROM MOMENTS OF RELIEF TO FEELINGS OF

IT WAS VERY STRANGE TO KNOW THAT UNTIL THEN I HAD
LIVED MY LIFE AS A DIFFERENT PERSON, WITH THOUGHTS
TAKEN UP BY BOYS AND FOOD AND HOW TO BE. I FEARED
I HAD MISSED OUT ON WHO I COULD HAVE BEEN HAD I
KNOWN EARLIER.

BUT SCREW THAT!

I DELETED TINDER – THANK GOD!

I STARTED DATING AGAIN — HELLO, LONDON!

ALL THINGS GAY AND BEAUTIFUL WERE SPILLING
INTO MY LIFE AND CHANGING MY HAIR, MY CLOTHES,
THE BOOKS I READ AND THE WAY I WORKED.
MY EXCITEMENT AND INSPIRATION DIMINISHED
ANY FEARS I HELD ABOUT WHAT I HAD LOST IN THOSE
LONG YEARS OF FALSE HETERO HELL.

I RETURNED TO MY UNIVERSITY FOR THE THIRD AND FINAL YEAR OF MY DEGREE AND IT WAS LIKE I'D STARTED OVER AGAIN. RATHER THAN SIMPLY CATCHING UP ON SUMMER EVENTS WITH MY FRIENDS, I GOT TO REINTRODUCE MYSELF AS THE 'REAL ME' BY COMING OUT IT FELT LIKE I'D BEEN WASHED CLEAN.

ELEVEN

THE FIRST DATE I EVER HAD WITH A WOMAN WENT
LIKE THIS:

WE AGREED TO MEET AT A PING-PONG
BAR AND I WORE MY NEW SHOES.

WHEN I ARRIVED WE GOT A PINT
AND SHE TOLD ME THAT I HAD
SO MANY DIFFERENT
HAIRSTYLES IN MY PROFILE
PHOTOS, SHE WASN'T SURE
WHAT I ACTUALLY
LOOKED LIKE.

WE HAD A FEW MORE DRINKS, ATE SOME PIZZA AND WALKED TO THE STATION.

SHE TEXTED ME TWO DAYS LATER SAYING THAT WE WEREN'T 'LOOKING FOR THE SAME THINGS'.

MY NEW SHOES HAD GIVEN ME BLISTERS.

SALT WATER FOR MY FEET →

BUT IT ONLY GOT WORSE WITH THE SECOND DATE ...

WE MET AT A WINE BAR AND SHE CALLED ME
A 'BABY GAY' WHEN SHE REALISED
I'D ONLY COME OUT RECENTLY.

SHE THEN ORDERED US A LONG AND EXPENSIVE TAXI
RIDE ACROSS LONDON TO A DIFFERENT BAR, WHERE WE
RAN INTO HER FRIENDS WHO WERE GOING TO A PARTY.

AFTER SOME MORE DRINKS SHE DECIDED SHE WAS GOING TO GO TO THAT PARTY AND THAT I SHOULDN'T COME WITH HER AS HER EX-GIRLFRIEND WOULD BE THERE AND SHE WANTED TO SCOPE IT OUT FIRST.

WE CAN MEET UP AGAIN LATER

IT'S 2 AM

I THREW UP WHEN I GOT HOME.

I WON'T LIE, I WAS SHOCKED.
I'D BEEN SO EXCITED ABOUT COMING OUT THAT I HAD
FORGOTTEN THAT THIS WOULDN'T MAKE DATING
SUDDENLY EASIER. I STILL HAD TO CONNECT WITH THE
PEOPLE I MET.

MY DATING EXPERIENCE HAD CONSISTED OF ME FORCING CONNECTIONS OR MISJUDGING THEM AS ROMANTIC. I'D HAD NO EXPERIENCE OF A GENUINE SPARK OF ATTRACTION.

I DIDN'T EVEN KNOW HOW TO FLIRT!

HOWEVER HARD IT WOULD GET,
I DECIDED THIS TIME I WOULD MAKE NO PLANS,
NO RULES OR REGULATIONS,
I WAS JUST GOING TO ENJOY MYSELF
AND KEEP TRYING.

AND THEN, I SAW HER.

TWELVE

I MET T AT A PUB IN NORTH LONDON.

WE SPOKE NON-STOP FOR FOUR HOURS,
AND AS THE PUB CLOSED SHE WALKED ME
TO MY BUS STOP AND WE TALKED ABOUT
OUR FAMILIES.

AS MY BUS ARRIVED TO GO HOME SHE HOPPED ON TO HER BIKE AND PEDALLED AWAY, CALLING GOODBYE OVER HER SHOULDER.

WE HAD SPOKEN ABOUT A BOOK WE WERE BOTH
READING AND THE WRITER WAS GIVING A TALK
IN A FEW WEEKS' TIME.

WE AGREED TO GO TOGETHER AS OUR SECOND DATE.

AFTER ABOUT FIVE DATES I KNEW IT WAS TIME
FOR US TO KISS, BUT I WAS SO SCARED!
I HAD KISSED GIRLS BEFORE, BUT NEVER IN
A ROMANTIC WAY. NEVER IN A WAY THAT WAS
MEANT TO MAKE THEM WANT TO KISS ME AGAIN.
AND I REALLY WANTED T TO KISS ME AGAIN!

AS WE WALKED BACK TO MY BUS STOP AFTER
OUR SIXTH DATE, I THINK WE BOTH KNEW IT WAS
THE MOMENT.

I SMILED THE WHOLE WAY HOME THAT NIGHT.

AFTER THAT WE BEGAN TO SEE EACH OTHER
REGULARLY EACH WEEK AND I STOPPED
ASKING OTHER GIRLS OUT ON DATES. THIS WASN'T
SOMETHING WE'D AGREED ON, IT JUST FELT RIGHT,
AND IT TURNED OUT SHE HAD MADE THE SAME CHOICE.

THIRTEEN

AFTER I GRADUATED FROM UNIVERSITY I WENT TO TORONTO FOR TWO WEEKS WITH MY PARENTS. I'D ALWAYS WANTED TO VISIT CANADA AND THIS WAS A TRIP I'D BEEN PLANNING FOR A LONG TIME.

BUT ONCE I WAS THERE I COULDN'T CONCENTRATE.

I MISSED T SO MUCH.
WE'D BEEN DATING FOR ALMOST NINE MONTHS
WITH HARDLY ANY TIME APART,
TWO WEEKS FELT LIKE A LIFETIME.

I REMEMBER WALKING DOWN THE STREET
WITH MY MUM ONE AFTERNOON OF OUR TRIP,
WHEN T SENT ME A DEMO FOR HER SONG.

SHE WAS SO RIGHT.

WE CALLED A FEW DAYS LATER AND BOOKED A TRIP
TO BARCELONA. I ENJOYED THE REST OF MY
HOLIDAY BUT WAS SECRETLY COUNTING
DOWN THE DAYS.

THE MOMENT I GOT BACK TO MY
HOUSE IN LONDON I THREW MY CLOTHES
IN A BAG, GRABBED THE PRESENTS I'D
BOUGHT FOR T AND JUMPED
IN A TAXI.

A FEW WEEKS LATER WE SET OFF ON OUR FIRST HOLIDAY TOGETHER.

ONE EVENING ON THAT TRIP, AFTER AN EVENTFUL DINNER
WHERE THE FOOD WAS COLD AND I'D KNOCKED OVER A
TABLE, SPILLING CHILLI SAUCE ACROSS THE FLOOR,
T ASKED ME TO BE HER GIRLFRIEND.

YEAH, WE'D BEEN DATING FOR NEARLY A YEAR BUT WE'D
AGREED TO TAKE THINGS AT OUR OWN PACE. IT FELT SO
PERFECT AND RIGHT WHEN T ASKED ME THAT NIGHT, WE
WALKED BACK HOME HOLDING HANDS,
LAUGHING ABOUT THE DINNER AND SINGING.

EPILOGUE

BEFORE I STARTED SEEING A COUNSELLOR I HAD TO
COMPLETE AN ASSESSMENT TO DETERMINE WHAT I
NEEDED. THE WOMAN WHO TOOK ME THROUGH IT WAS
SCOTTISH WITH FRECKLES AND HAD
FLUFFY BROWN HAIR.

I CAN'T REMEMBER EVERYTHING SHE ASKED ME BUT ONE
OF THE QUESTIONS ALWAYS STUCK IN MY MIND
AFTERWARDS.
SHE SAID:

AND I SAID:

ORANGE LIKE MY HAIR — ORANGE LIKE THE SUN SEEN THROUGH CLOSED EYELIDS.

WHEN I CAME OUT THAT FINAL
TIME IN MY ROOM, THE BIGGEST
KNOT I HAVE EVER CARRIED
IN MY LIFE CAME UNDONE.

OF COURSE, THERE
HAVE SINCE BEEN
— THERE ARE —
AND THERE WILL BE
OTHER KNOTS...

BUT WHEN I REALISED HOW I NEEDED TO LIVE
MY LIFE, I BECAME MORE FEARLESS ABOUT
THEM ALL.